HomeBuilders *Couples Series*®

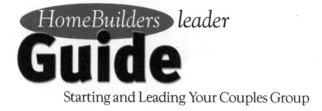

HomeBuilders *leader*
Guide

Starting and Leading Your Couples Group

By Drew and Kit Coons

*"Unless the Lord
builds the house,
its builders
labor in vain"
(Psalm 127:1a).*

FAMILYLIFE™
Bringing Timeless Principles Home
Little Rock, Arkansas

Loveland, Colorado

Group's R.E.A.L. Guarantee to you:

Every Group resource incorporates our R.E.A.L. approach to ministry—
a unique philosophy that results in long-term retention and life
transformation. It's ministry that's:

This is EARL.
He's R.E.A.L.
mixed-up.
(Get it?)

Relational
Because student-to-student interaction enhances learning and builds Christian friendships.

Experiential
Because what students experience sticks with them up to 9 times longer than what they simply hear or read.

Applicable
Because the aim of Christian education is to be both hearers and doers of the Word.

Learner-based
Because students learn more and retain it longer when the process is designed according to how they learn best.

HomeBuilders Leader Guide

Visit our Web site: **www.grouppublishing.com**

Credits

Editor: Matt Lockhart
Creative Development Editor: Paul Woods
Chief Creative Officer: Joani Schultz
Copy Editor: Dena Twinem
Art Director: Jenette L. McEntire
Cover Art Director: Jeff A. Storm
Computer Graphic Artist: Anita M. Cook
Cover Photographer: Tony Stone Images
Illustrator: Ken Jacobsen
Production Manager: Peggy Naylor

ISBN 0-7644-2249-9
10 9 8   09 08 07 06 05 04 03 02

Printed in the United States of America.

How to Let the Lord Build Your House
and not labor in vain

•

The HomeBuilders Couples Series®: A small-group Bible study dedicated to making your family all that God intended.

FamilyLife is a division of Campus Crusade for Christ International, an evangelical Christian organization founded in 1951 by Bill Bright. FamilyLife was started in 1976 to help fulfill the Great Commission by strengthening marriages and families and then equipping them to go to the world with the gospel of Jesus Christ. The FamilyLife Marriage Conference is held in most major cities throughout the United States and is one of the fastest-growing marriage conferences in America today. "FamilyLife Today," a daily radio program hosted by Dennis Rainey, is heard on hundreds of stations across the country. Information on all resources offered by FamilyLife may by obtained by contacting us at the address, telephone number, or World Wide Web site listed below.

Dennis Rainey, Executive Director
FamilyLife
P.O. Box 8220
Little Rock, AR 72221-8220
1-800-FL-TODAY
www.familylife.com

A division of Campus Crusade for Christ International
Bill Bright, Founder and President

HOMEBUILDERS LEADER GUIDE

Contents

Are You Ready to Become a HomeBuilder?

by Dennis Rainey

●

Their marriage was dead and buried. It had limped along for nearly thirty years, but they no longer communicated except to, in the wife's words, "growl at each other." Their hearts were cold and hard.

They divorced, and the woman moved across the country to start a new life. She began attending a church where she understood the gospel for the first time and made a faith commitment to Christ. Some friends invited her to attend a home Bible study and, on the first evening she was there, a HomeBuilders Couples Series® study was introduced.

"I was still so very angry over the way my marriage had ended, and with my life in general," the woman wrote, "but something was beginning to happen inside of me. For the first time in thirty years, I was able to understand what was missing from our marriage. We did not have personal relationships with Jesus Christ. The seed was planted that night, but I still fought against the idea of getting back with my former husband."

Through a HomeBuilders Couples Series study, the woman read the Bible and understood it in a way she had never experienced before. She wrote to her ex-husband to tell him what she was learning, and was surprised to receive a phone call.

For the first time they talked about what God wanted to do in their marriage.

The next week he flew out and attended one of the HomeBuilders sessions. They read the Bible together and answered as many questions in the study material as they could. That weekend he committed his life to Jesus Christ as well, and when he asked her to remarry him, she said, "Yes!"

That is just one of hundreds of stories I could tell about the power of the HomeBuilders Couples Series in the lives of married couples. If you're looking for an opportunity to help other couples grow closer to God and to each other—and improve your own marriage in the process—HomeBuilders is for you!

Like never before, married couples are hungry for answers. They want to know what can help them build the type of relationship they dreamed of before they married. They want to know how to defeat isolation and enjoy oneness. And, though some may not know it, they long to grow closer to God and know how the truth of his Word can transform their lives.

We began this series because we saw that one of the most effective ways for married couples to learn God's principles for marriage is in the context of a small group. In a culture where divorce is commonplace, where fewer and fewer children grow up observing good role models for how to keep a marriage together, couples now, more than ever, need ongoing encouragement to remain committed to their marriage vows.

HomeBuilders studies work because:

1. *They stimulate couples to examine what Scripture says about how to construct a solid, satisfying marriage.* Couples not only learn principles, but are also motivated to take specific actions to apply them in their marriages.

2. *They help couples address penetrating questions about their marriages.* Jim Diffee, a lay leader in the Evangelical Community Church of Jackson, Tennessee, wrote in Discipleship Journal about the HomeBuilders Couples Series, "This study is both proactive and challenging. Even though I've been a Christian for sixteen years and have been married for more than eight, I found myself being challenged to ask some hard questions and to re-evaluate my marriage in light of what Scripture has to say."

3. *They encourage couples to interact with each other.* The relaxed surrounding of a home study lends itself well to the informal interaction of a small group. People are more inclined to open up in the nonthreatening environment of a home. The group becomes a place where people slow down and experience community with others. We not only find out what's going on in one another's lives, but we can also be affirmed and develop meaningful relationships with others. And it encourages mutual accountability, where the group helps each other as they seek to follow God and obey his Word.

4. *They make it easy for couples to minister to couples.* God is not dependent on paid professionals or highly-trained technicians to do his work. Of course, he uses well-trained professionals, but he also works through "average," available people.

Some of the best advice I ever received was given by a good friend as we were driving home from a fishing trip. I asked him, "What would you do if you had a fast-growing family ministry and were trying to help the church strengthen families?"

I'll never forget his words spoken in the darkness of the car: "I would take the message and ministry out of the hands of the professionals and put them into the hands of the people."

That's what we've done. In thousands of communities, husbands and wives are leading HomeBuilders groups and having an impact in the lives of other couples.

Some friends of ours, Roy and Susan Milam, have been true difference-makers in their community. Roy recalls, "A friend challenged me with words I'll never forget: 'Life is not a dress rehearsal. If you really want to make a difference in this world, maybe you ought to think about leading a HomeBuilders group.' "

Roy and his wife saw their marriage and others' marriages transformed as they led their first group. "Husbands and wives began communicating about issues they had never discussed," Roy says. "Couples who were angry and resentful became supportive and loving. We saw God work in lots of wonderful ways through HomeBuilders."

5. *Leading a study requires little preparation.* It's a short-term commitment (six to seven weeks), and you don't have to be an expert to lead.

6. *Those who lead a group benefit from the experience.* Over and over we hear leaders tell us that HomeBuilders studies have helped them grow in their marriages. One couple, Bob and Kerri Cole, initially hesitated to lead a HomeBuilders group because they didn't feel qualified. Eventually they tried it, and enjoyed it so much they ended up leading groups for years.

When they looked back at what they had written in the workbooks of some of their early studies, they "realized how big some of the issues were—they represented huge thorns in our marriage," Kerri says. "The Lord not only repaired damage that seemed irreparable, but also removed the pain from our memories...Each time we do a study, there are deeper levels of intimacy to be enjoyed."

Are you ready to become a HomeBuilder? This *HomeBuilders Leader Guide* by Drew and Kit Coons will help you get started. Drew and Kit have been involved with HomeBuilders groups since 1989 and have started over four hundred different groups. No one can better share with you the basics of leading a HomeBuilders group.

I need to warn you, however, that leading a HomeBuilders group can be addictive. Once you get started, you will begin to see how God works in your lives, in your marriage, and in the lives of your group members. Nothing is more exciting!

Attention HomeBuilders Leaders

FamilyLife invites you to register your HomeBuilders group. Your registration connects you to the HomeBuilders Leadership Network, a worldwide movement of couples who are using HomeBuilders to strengthen marriages and families in their communities. You'll receive the latest news about HomeBuilders and other ministry opportunities to help strengthen marriages and families in your community. As the HomeBuilders Leadership Network grows, we will offer additional resources such as online training, prayer requests, and chat with authors. There is no cost or obligation to register; simply go to www.familylife.com/homebuilders.

Chapter One

You Can Lead a HomeBuilders Group

Can an average couple be used by God to have a significant impact with families? Yes!

Without any special marriage leadership training, we began a small-group study in 1989 using the HomeBuilders Couples Series. Over the years, God has transformed marriages before our eyes, and many people have come to know Jesus Christ in a personal way. And though we had a good, stable marriage, we were thrilled to see God take it to an even higher level.

God calls all of us who are his disciples to make a real difference in others' lives. Yet many people are held back by a lack of vision and a failure to develop ministry skills.

Believe us, the world will be a better place if you allow God to share his blueprints for marriage through you. You can make a real difference in the lives of families.

Some common concerns about leading a HomeBuilders group

"I don't think I have enough time."

Many potential leaders feel pressured by time—there just doesn't seem to be enough time to do all they want. Believe it or not, HomeBuilders can actually be a timesaver. This one activity can combine a number of your top priorities. It gives you the opportunity to:

- invest in your marriage relationship,

- study the Bible,

- improve your character in Christ,

- have fun and make friends,

- serve your church,

- reach out to other people with the love of Christ, and

- strengthen your family by strengthening your marriage.

You also won't need to spend a lot of time preparing to lead a session. In each study there are Leader's Notes for each session that are designed to help make preparing quick and easy. And even the time you spend in preparation is valuable because it gives you the opportunity to think and pray for your group and about the Scriptures and issues you'll be studying.

"I don't have any training or experience in leading a small group."

No problem. "First timers" make some of the best leaders. In the process of going through the study, you'll receive some of the best training there is—on the job! HomeBuilders studies are written so that the group leader just needs to ask the questions. You don't need to be an accomplished Bible teacher to lead a HomeBuilders group. In fact, your role is that of *facilitator*, not lecturer. The main function of a facilitator is to keep the discussion moving and to provide an environment of openness, warmth, and acceptance of others. If you can do that, you can lead a HomeBuilders group.

If you are still unsure about leading a group, consider co-leading with another couple. Together you can divide the responsibilities and trust God to work in your lives to help other couples.

"How can we lead a group about improving marriage when we're still working through issues in our own marriage?"

The best leaders are couples who are willing to share their successes and admit to weaknesses while trying to have a better marriage. Unless you and your spouse are working through severe problems in your relationship, chances are you can do a good job of leading other married couples. Let them know from the outset that you are learning just as they are.

One leader told us, "We have now led HomeBuilders Groups for three years. You don't lead the group as much as you guide it. You're not a counselor; you're just another married couple that wants to see marriages work."

"This is not my first marriage. Why would anyone listen to me?"

When it comes to marriage enrichment, those who have experienced a failed marriage may feel unqualified. They may think that nobody will listen to their experiences or insight. This is far from true. Couples who have suffered the heartbreak of a divorce often go the extra mile to prevent this from happening to others. They frequently make outstanding leaders. God has greatly used many couples who have a divorce in their background.

What helps make an excellent HomeBuilders leader?

1. *A desire to allow God to work in and through your life as you reach out to others.* Galatians 5:22-23 tells us that "the fruit of the Spirit is love, joy, peace, patience, kindness, goodness, faithfulness, gentleness and self-control." It's impossible to live the Christian life in your own power.

To lead a group effectively, it is more important to live by the Spirit than to have a seminary education. Every HomeBuilders group is different. There is no way to train for or anticipate every situation and how to deal with it. But the Holy Spirit can and will give you wisdom in every situation.

Jesus promised his disciples in Luke 12:12 that "the Holy Spirit will teach you at that time what you should say." Many HomeBuilders leaders find that, in the middle of a discussion, they suddenly think of a new way to illustrate a certain truth or to emphasize an important point. And later they discover their comment was exactly what the members of that group needed. At other times the Holy Spirit will lead them to keep silent and allow the group members to minister to each other.

2. *A commitment to your marriage and a desire to invest in its growth.* This doesn't mean that your own marriage is perfect, just that you are committed to it and willing to work to make it better. Leading a HomeBuilders group means that you will spend time every week as a couple talking about how the Scriptures apply to your lives. Nothing will help you grow more.

We also encourage couples to use their groups to establish accountability to stay committed to their spouses. We made a special commitment several years ago. We had seen one too many Christians fail morally. I (Drew) went to the men I worked with and requested, "If you see me flirting with a woman, or having any involvement that could even lead to trouble, I want you to tell Kit." Now there's a big incentive!

3. *A desire to love and encourage people.* Perhaps no skill is more important in leading a volunteer ministry than the ability to encourage others. And all of us need encouragement. We suggest you start by practicing on your spouse.

Some people who join a group can be difficult to love and encourage. Since we know loving them is God's will, we can by faith ask God to give us his love for that person. 1 John 5:14-15 guarantees that he will give us that love in answer to our prayer.

Remember that God's love is much more than feelings. It may take time for your feelings to change. To accelerate the process, do something nice for a "difficult" person, secretly if possible. Find something positive about him or her and concentrate on it. You'll find God has kept his promise as your feelings start to change.

4. *A willingness to practice hospitality.* There's something special about inviting guests into your home. You don't need a fancy house (or even a neat house) or expensive food to serve. What you do need is to honor and value your guests.

God-honoring hospitality can extend well beyond our homes. It can be any act of thoughtfulness that demonstrates how

much we value others. Remembering birthdays, a willingness to help out, and encouraging notes are all types of hospitality. If Jesus cared enough to die for us, we should be
able to go out of our way to serve those around us and
demonstrate his love.

5. *A desire to minister as a couple.* "My wife always supported
my ministry," a pastor said. "She played the piano and
attended all the classes I taught. But when we started co-
leading a HomeBuilders study, it was different." He went
on to describe how much fun it was and how well the couples in the study were responding. Clearly he had discovered a wonderful resource in his own wife.

Unfortunately, the concept of working together isn't very pop-
ular in our "be-your-own-person" culture. Individualism is
valued over partnership. But in marriage, God wants us to
need one another, to trust one another, and to work together
for common goals. We believe one great unrealized opportunity in many churches is that of husbands and wives ministering
together. With HomeBuilders you have that opportunity.

Some challenges of ministering together

If you play tennis, you know that mixed doubles can test any
relationship! Teamwork is more than just being on the same
court—a lesson I (Drew) learned the hard way. After Kit and I
started playing together, I started pointing out mistakes she was
making and ways to improve her game. The more I criticized
her, the worse she played.

Things went from bad to worse. As I continued criticizing
the way she played, Kit got so bad that I told her, "Serve the

ball and step off the court. I'll play the shots by myself."

As much as I wanted to win, I discovered I could not do it alone. During that particularly disastrous match, I made a startling discovery: Kit's play was directly related to the way I treated her. Whenever I criticized her, she was awful. But when I encouraged her—when she was having fun—her confidence soared and she was great. From then on, playing with Kit was the most fun I ever had in tennis.

We learned the same lesson as we started developing a HomeBuilders ministry, as well as promoting FamilyLife Marriage Conferences. It was tough. There was tremendous temptation to criticize one another when the pressure was on. But once we learned how to honor and encourage one another, our work together became something we enjoyed—something we shared. And that, we've found, is the most important thing about developing a ministry together.

Another thing we've learned is how to use our differences to make our partnership stronger. The Bible says, "Two are better than one, because they have a good return for their work: If one falls down, his friend can help him up. But pity the man who falls and has no one to help him up!" (Ecclesiastes 4:9-10).

All couples have major differences. God knows that when he puts us together. In fact, the greater our differences, the stronger we can become as a team.

When we lead a HomeBuilders group, one way we work as a team is by dividing the preparation and cleanup duties. Kit prepares a dessert for the group to enjoy, while I help straighten up the house and set up chairs for the meeting. We try to have everything finished so we will both be free to spend time with the couples when they arrive. Afterward we clean up together.

During the study, we often take turns leading different sections. While one is leading, the other can be extra sensitive to what God may be doing in the hearts of the people in the group.

We would like you to think of the HomeBuilders Couples Series as a ministry belonging to both of you. Together you can have a unique influence in the lives of other couples. At the same time, you'll be strengthening your own relationship as husband and wife through the biblical applications in the studies and by trusting God as together you serve others.

●

I had never led a group before in my life. We went to the pastor and he gave us his blessing to start a group with five other couples. We were terrified, especially having a church elder and his wife join us. Later, this couple shared that they had never, in thirty-five years of marriage, discussed some of the issues that were covered in our group. There is no reason not to do a HomeBuilders study. You don't have to be a Bible teacher or scholar because these studies make it easy for anybody.

Ken and Irma Morris

Chapter Two

Starting a HomeBuilders Group

Once you decide to begin a HomeBuilders study, the next question is, "Where should we start?" For many of you, the natural place to begin is in your church.

One couple attended a FamilyLife Marriage Conference and heard about the HomeBuilders Couples Series. A few days later, they met with the Christian education board at their church and presented the idea of starting a HomeBuilders group. The board agreed, and they began using it in a Sunday school class. A wide range of couples attended the class, and it was a success from the start.

If you are interested in starting HomeBuilders in your church, approach your pastor or Christian education director and volunteer to lead a group.

Remember that a pastor is very busy. Don't just leave the material on your pastor's desk with a note saying HomeBuilders would be good for the church. Instead, show your pastor a copy of the study and share your desire to start a HomeBuilders group. Explain how the principles from the study have affected your life, and share how churches can use HomeBuilders in a variety of ways. Show a copy of the HomeBuilders promotional video (for a copy, call 1-800-FL-TODAY). Offer to take leadership in organizing HomeBuilders. Make it clear you will do the work.

Here are a few points you can share with your pastor about how HomeBuilders can benefit a church:

- It can help decrease a pastor's counseling load.
- It helps build marriages and families.
- It reclaims troubled marriages.
- It provides a small-group strategy.
- It equips members of the congregation to have a life-changing ministry.
- It provides a tool to reach out to non-Christians and unchurched couples.
- It builds relationships between couples.
- It helps church members become excited about their relationships with God.

You can introduce HomeBuilders into a church in several settings:

Small groups: Churches most frequently use HomeBuilders in small groups. If small groups already exist at your church, talk with the person who makes decisions on the curriculum. If there are no small groups currently meeting, you could offer to organize a "pilot project" and begin with one or two groups.

Retreats or weekend emphasis: A church or Sunday school class often sets aside a weekend to emphasize strong marriages. This provides a great setting to share a series of HomeBuilders sessions. You can enhance the weekend by holding it at a retreat center or lodge. Including games and fun activities in the schedule can make the weekend even more special.

Sunday school: Many group leaders have successfully used HomeBuilders studies in a Sunday school class. One couple called it "the most practical material we have ever used in our Sunday school—it forces couples to open up."

Promoting HomeBuilders in the church

Once you receive permission to start a group in your church, you'll want to promote it.

Consider the following ideas:

- Send invitations to church members and neighbors.

- Advertise in the church bulletin, newsletter, or fliers.

- Conduct an introductory meeting to demonstrate the effectiveness and fun of HomeBuilders. Show the HomeBuilders promotional video.

- Ask your pastor to endorse HomeBuilders from the pulpit.

- Use sign-up sheets.

Forming other types of HomeBuilders groups

We have found that starting HomeBuilders groups outside a church is sometimes more difficult, but extremely rewarding. Steve and Dianne Robinson, for example, started a HomeBuilders group in their neighborhood in Marietta, Georgia. For some time they had been troubled by the needs of families in their neighborhood. Going door to door, they passed out nearly three hundred fliers inviting neighbors to come to their home for dessert and to hear about the study. Out of the three hundred invitations, fourteen couples showed up; and out of the fourteen couples, ten decided to participate in Steve and Dianne's HomeBuilders group. And at least half of them started attending church with Steve and Dianne as a result of attending the study.

Our experience indicates those most likely to respond to your invitation are couples with whom you already have some kind of relationship or affiliation. Pray about reaching your neighbors or work associates with a HomeBuilders group. Or possibly parents from your children's schools or athletic teams. Brainstorm with your spouse and make a list of those to invite.

While a positive response may be greater among those you know, don't limit your group to friends. Issues associated with marriage and family are of deep concern for most couples. You may be surprised by who expresses interest in learning more about God's blueprints for marriage. Don't limit yourselves by denominational backgrounds. Often the strongest and most meaningful groups are composed of couples from widely differing backgrounds.

A personal invitation is always better than just a written one. A written invitation followed by a call or personal visit is best. You may want to host a small event to build interest in HomeBuilders. A neighborhood cookout or potluck can be an excellent occasion to introduce others to HomeBuilders. A romantic dinner party at a restaurant or hotel with a brief biblical message on marriage is another good way to get couples interested. (Be sure to tell couples about the topic of the message when you're inviting them.)

When you introduce HomeBuilders to your neighbors or friends, communicate the following:

1. Describe what the HomeBuilders Couples Series is like in terms they can understand. Talk about the need for couples to invest in their marriages and to learn how to relate to one another better.

2. Share from your personal experience how these principles

have affected your marriage, and how you benefited from getting to know other couples.

3. Communicate these essential facts:

- when you will meet,
- where you will meet (and if refreshments will be served),
- what time you will start and finish,
- how many weeks the study will last, and
- what you will be studying.

4. Ask for two commitments on the part of the people who want to attend the HomeBuilders sessions: try to come to every session, and try to complete the "homework" (HomeBuilders Projects) in between the sessions.

5. For those who indicate they will "think about it," tell them you will call in a few days for their decision. And be sure to keep your word.

Pray that God will lead you to people who need to build their marriages, and be courageous as you challenge them to join. For many couples, you will offer their only glimpse of what God has to say about marriage and how they can effectively relate to one another to build a satisfying and God-honoring relationship.

Forming groups from FamilyLife Marriage Conference alumni

Nobody can apply or even absorb all they hear at a FamilyLife Marriage Conference. That's one reason conference guests are encouraged to join or to lead a HomeBuilders group. It gives them an opportunity to discuss God's principles for marriage with other couples in a small-group setting. And it also provides a great tool for them to reach into the homes of millions of couples who will never attend a conference.

Call FamilyLife (1-800-FL-TODAY) for the name and phone number of the nearest local city ministry director, and then contact the director to find out if anyone is forming HomeBuilders groups from conference alumni. If not, get a list of couples who expressed an interest in HomeBuilders at the latest conference in your area, and call them.

Forming outreach groups

A HomeBuilders study can be an effective outreach tool because so many people are experiencing problems in their marriages and families. People who have no religious affiliation or background can feel comfortable in these groups because they are formed around the topic of marriage. People are hungry for real solutions to their problems.

We've seen several individuals make commitments to Christ as a result of a study. One man and woman who were unmarried but living together attended a HomeBuilders group. As a result, he became a Christian and moved out. Eventually they were married and then he moved back in!

HomeBuilders groups can be especially effective for reaching out to couples who profess faith in Christ but don't seem spiritually committed. In fact, we've heard story after story of individuals and marriages finding new spiritual vitality through these groups.

One special caution: Many churches have used HomeBuilders as an outreach, but are disappointed when some couples go elsewhere after the group ends. Unchurched couples may become interested in spiritual things through HomeBuilders, but when it's time to choose a church they may seek one similar to the one in which they grew up. Our advice is to be joyful in ministering to others without any expectations other than God's promise to change lives through biblical principles. Reach out in the power of the Spirit, and let God work on their hearts.

For more information on using HomeBuilders to reach out to non-Christians, be sure to read chapter 6, "Using HomeBuilders for Outreach."

HomeBuilders studies have helped our church to be intentional about a marriage and family ministry. We use HomeBuilders primarily to give couples preventative tools and guidelines to strengthen their relationship before a crisis. But HomeBuilders is also part of our counseling ministry. We ask every couple who requests counseling to join an ongoing group. We've had as many as fifteen groups going at once. But a church could start with just one group and grow with it. We use HomeBuilders in our small-group ministry in couples' homes and also in Sunday school. We start a group any time or place couples want to meet. The materials are very flexible and allow you to use them many ways.

Pastor Gene Tyson

Chapter Three

Frequently Asked Questions About Leading a Group

How many couples should be in a group?

Ideally, four to eight couples (including you and your spouse). The fewer the number of couples, the more the group is subject to canceling a meeting if one or two couples are unable to attend a given session.

Having more than eight couples may reduce the quality of relationships that can grow between the couples involved. However, even in very large groups there can still be opportunities for couples to interact with other couples in the group. You can enhance interaction by breaking down portions of the discussion into smaller groups.

Should we form a group with people our age?

Leading the group may be easier if your group is made up of couples at similar stages in their relationships. The more the group has in common, the easier it will be for people to identify with one another and open up and share. However, it can be helpful for a couple to gain a fresh viewpoint on marriage by interacting with a couple who has significantly different experiences. And the principles in HomeBuilders are beneficial to couples at any stage in marriage. In other words, if a couple is interested in building and maintaining a strong marriage, this study is for them.

What is the best setting for a group meeting?

The best setting will depend on what type of group you want. In some cases, you will meet at a church or another public place. But in general, inviting couples to your home is easier and friendlier than trying to get them to come to your church. Even church groups enjoy meeting in someone's home.

You need to have a place where everyone can sit comfortably and see and hear each other. If your home will not work, see if another couple in the group is willing to host the sessions. Rotating to different members' homes can work as well.

What time schedule should we follow?

Whether you meet weekly or biweekly will depend on what type of group you are forming. If this will be a church-based group, you probably will need to conform to your church Sunday school or small-group schedule. If it's another type of group, you and your spouse will need to decide what's best.

Each session in a HomeBuilders study usually takes about ninety minutes to complete. However, to allow for refreshments and a time of informal fellowship, we recommend planning to meet for two hours. This will allow you to move through the study at a more relaxed pace. If you plan to use this study in a Sunday school setting, refer to the section "Leading HomeBuilders in Sunday school" at the end of chapter 4. This will provide you some options on adapting the material for a class.

When you invite people to your group, tell them to plan on two hours. This avoids having people rush off and not get acquainted. Regardless of the time frame, be sure to follow one of the cardinal rules of a good group: Start *and* end on time. People's time is valuable, and your group will appreciate you being respectful of this.

What about refreshments?

Many groups choose to serve refreshments to help create an environment of fellowship. If you plan on doing this, here are a couple of suggestions to consider. (1) For the first session (or two) you should provide the refreshments and then allow the group to be involved by having people sign up to bring them to future sessions. (2) You may want to save refreshments until after the discussion time. Otherwise, you may delay your start and not get finished. Also, those who may need to leave early can do so without missing the discussion. (3) Another option is to start the group with a short time of informal fellowship and refreshments (fifteen minutes), then move into the study. This way, if couples are late, they only miss the food and don't disrupt the study. However, be sure to still end on time, and to allow anyone who needs to leave right away to do so gracefully.

What about child care?

It is important that your group focus on the study material without distractions and interruptions from children. Discourage couples from bringing small children unless you are providing baby-sitting at your home. Ask your group what works best for them. Some may prefer to have their own baby sitter. Others may find that paying for a baby sitter every week is too costly.

It's also important that your child care be dependable. Some couples will not be able to commit to every group session if child care is not provided. Here are some suggestions:

- Arrange baby-sitting in one house and hold the study in another.

- Pool resources to hire a baby sitter.

- Contact your youth pastor for referrals or perhaps a youth service project.

- Ask if any couples have older children who would be able to baby-sit.

- Use available child care or church facilities when the nursery is open.

Whatever you do, encourage the group as a whole to come to a mutual decision about child care.

What about prayer?

An important part of a HomeBuilders group is prayer. In preparing for a session, one of the best things you can do is to pray for each person in the group. In leading a group, you need to be sensitive to the level of comfort the people in the group have toward praying aloud. Never call on people to pray aloud without first knowing if they are comfortable doing this. Consider using a creative approach to leading prayer, such as modeling prayer, calling for volunteers, letting people pray silently, and letting people state their prayers in the form of finishing a sentence.

A prayer list can be helpful. You should lead prayer time, but allow another couple the opportunity to create, update, and distribute prayer lists.

The HomeBuilders class turned everything around in our relationship. It was a real miracle. The walls came down and the masks came off. We were able to discuss matters we had swept under the rug years ago that our enemy was consistently using to destroy the love God had designed for us since the beginning of time. It has changed the entire way we live and communicate.

The HomeBuilders class really works. Here is why: HomeBuilders not only shows you why and tells you how, it also teaches a way to alter your lifestyle so these great truths become a part of everyday living.

We have truly overcome isolation and are building toward oneness in our marriage. We have learned how to yield to God and the leading of his Holy Spirit instead of our own selfish desires.

We have made our marriage a priority through submission and respect for each other...the romance is back and the intimacy is growing every day. It's absolutely the best thing that has ever happened to us since becoming Christians eighteen years ago.

Alan and Lanette Hauge

Chapter Four

Leading a HomeBuilders Session

Each session in every study is comprised of the following categories: Warm-Up, Blueprints, Wrap-Up, and HomeBuilders Project.

Warm-Up (15 minutes)

The purpose of Warm-Up is to help people unwind from a busy day and get to know each other better. Typically, the first point in Warm-Up is an exercise that is meant to be fun while introducing the topic of the session. The ability to share in fun with others is important in building relationships. Another component of Warm-Up is the Project Report (except in session one), which is designed to provide accountability in relation to the HomeBuilders Project that is to be completed by couples between sessions. Beware of using too much time in Warm-Up and not having enough time for the remainder of the study.

Blueprints (60 minutes)

This is the heart of the study. In this category, people answer pertinent questions related to the topic of study and look to God's Word for understanding. Some of the questions are designed to be answered by couples, some in subgroups, and some in the group at large. There are notes in the margin or instructions within a question that designate these groupings.

We suggest simply reading Blueprints questions aloud to the group members and wait for them to answer. Don't be afraid of silence that may feel awkward, especially at first. But be prepared to get the discussion moving by sharing examples from your own lives whenever it's appropriate.

Wrap-Up (15 minutes)

This category serves to "bring home the point" and wind down a session in an appropriate fashion.

Also, within Wrap-Up, couples are encouraged to take a minute and "Make a Date" with their spouse for that week. They are encouraged to use their date to do their HomeBuilders Project.

HomeBuilders Project (60 minutes)

This project, to be completed with your spouse in between group sessions, is the unique application step in a HomeBuilders study.

Within most HomeBuilders Projects there are three sections: (1) As a Couple—a brief exercise designed to get the date started, (2) Individually—a section of questions for husbands and wives to answer separately, and (3) Interact as a Couple—an opportunity for couples to share their answers with each other and make application in their lives.

Doing the HomeBuilders Project is vitally important; it will multiply the impact of the HomeBuilders experience. Emphasize that this is not homework to get a passing grade, but a highly enjoyable time of interaction that will improve communication and understanding for each couple.

In addition to the prior regular features, there will occasionally be an activity that is labeled "For Extra Impact." The purpose of these activities is to provide a more active or visual way to help make a particular point. Be mindful that within a group people have different learning styles. While most of what is presented is verbal, a visual or active exercise now and again is helpful to engage more of the senses and appeal to people who learn best by seeing, touching, and doing.

Preparing to lead a session

The sessions in the HomeBuilders studies have been designed to be easily led without a lot of preparation time. However, you should review each session before your group meeting. Familiarize yourself with the important concepts you'll be studying, and look up each Bible verse. You'll also want to review the Leader's Notes in the back of the study for the session you are preparing to lead. These notes are designed to help you prepare quickly and easily. The Leader's Notes cover the following points.

Objectives

The purpose of the objectives is to help focus the issues that will be presented in a given session.

Notes and Tips

This section will relate any general comments in regard to the session. The information here should be viewed as ideas, helps, and suggestions. You may want to create a checklist of things you want to be sure to do in a given session.

Commentary

Included in this section are notes that relate specifically to a given Blueprints question. Not all Blueprints questions in a session will have an accompanying commentary note. The questions that do have related commentary are designated by number (for example, Blueprints question 5 in session one would correspond to number 5 in the Commentary section of session one Leader's Notes).

Additional considerations

If you are co-leading with your spouse, or with another couple, decide who will be leading each part. In many groups, it's not unusual for one person to serve as the primary leader throughout. But in some situations, sharing leadership between a husband and wife can be very effective. It allows the other spouse time to be sensitive to the needs of the various group members.

As you prepare for each session, you'll find that some questions are more relevant to your group than others. Pace your study in such a way that the questions that most need to be addressed are not rushed. Also, think through the questions that call for sharing personal experiences. Decide on some applications or examples you can share for each of these questions. Those from your own life are most effective. Check them out with your spouse first.

You are the leader of your group, and you know the needs of the individual couples best. But keep in mind that the Holy Spirit may have an agenda that you don't realize in advance. Proverbs 16:9 says, "In his heart a man plans his course, but the Lord determines his steps." Do your best to prepare, and pray for the session, and then leave the results to God.

Beginning the session

It is important to start at, or near, the announced time. Otherwise, you'll find it difficult to end on time. We've also found that some couples will arrive at your group later and later if you don't establish from the very outset that your group starts on time. In the first session, you should share these ground rules:

• Don't share anything that would embarrass your spouse.

• You may pass on any question you don't want to answer.

• If possible, plan to complete the HomeBuilders Project as a couple between group sessions.

(These ground rules are also included in the introduction of each of the HomeBuilders Couples Series courses.)

The seating arrangement is very important to facilitate discussion and involvement. Use a large room where everyone can sit and see each other. If your home will not work, see if another couple in the group is willing to serve as host. Also, avoid letting couples or individuals sit outside the group; they will not feel included. The diagrams on the next page illustrate the best group dynamics for how to lead a HomeBuilders group.

NOT THIS:

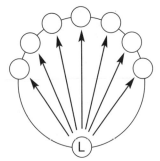

The leader doing all the talking and
the people all the listening.

OR THIS:

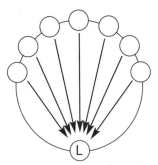

The members responding only to
the leader in answering questions.

BUT THIS:

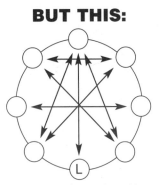

Group members interacting with each
other; the leader guiding the discussion.

The questions in the session are written to force group members to explore the Scriptures together and think about how to apply God's truth to their lives. Usually the group will learn from each other, and will not need much guidance from you.

Ending the session

You may want to end the session with a time of prayer. Remember to be careful selecting who you ask to pray since many people don't feel comfortable praying publicly. Consider using some of the methods suggested in chapter 3, under the question, "What about prayer?"

Remind couples to complete the HomeBuilders Project before the next session. Frequently God uses these projects to change lives more than anything else.

Between sessions

It's a good idea to contact couples by phone, e-mail, or a postcard in between each session; this is especially important if you're meeting biweekly. This helps to build a rapport or bond between the participants and the group. You will find that fewer couples drop out of the group if you maintain this bond.

Encourage activities together outside of the group sessions. Many groups set a night to go out for dinner together or some other fun activity. This helps couples to make friends. Relationships encourage everyone to be accountable to one another to do the assignments and apply the biblical principles to their own marriages. It also gives struggling couples the benefit of role models and mentors.

Leading HomeBuilders in Sunday school

Although the sessions generally run longer in a HomeBuilders study (ninety minutes) than the typical Sunday school class (sixty minutes), there are a couple of options for using this material in a class setting.

One option is to spend two classes on each session. This will give you time to cover all the material in a given session. Another option is to concentrate your class time on the part of the HomeBuilders session called Blueprints. Blueprints is the heart of the study and is designed to run for one hour.

When using HomeBuilders in Sunday school, remember that the strength of the HomeBuilders experience is in the small-group interaction between couples. Split the class into smaller groups if necessary; we recommend groups of three to four couples.

Remember, your role is that of *facilitator*, not teacher. Many Sunday school classes follow a lecture format and use little small-group interaction. You should seek to guide your group to discover the truth rather than teaching it yourself.

●

A precious couple came across our path. They took the study and we invited them to become leaders. The husband said, "Oh you don't understand, we can't do that." We explained that all you have to do is agree to be facilitator. Just keep the group moving forward in the information. And your own marriage will be richly blessed. Soon after they started a group, they called to tell us they would have divorced if they hadn't grown out of their isolation because of the HomeBuilders group.

Tazwell and Bonita Thorton

Dealing With Challenges in Your Group

How do I handle couples with severe marital problems?

When you open your home and your lives to other couples, God can use you in amazing ways. A husband and wife with severe marital problems may come to your group and receive the encouragement and help they need to turn their marriage around. Often they are looking for a wise friend and a listening ear.

At the same time, you'll need to make prayerful decisions about how much you'll be involved in the lives of couples with severe problems. While we encourage you to minister to them and help them as much as you feel you can, you are not responsible to be their counselors; in many cases one of the best steps you can take is to refer them to a pastor or a professional counselor. That's especially important if you become aware of underlying issues such as infidelity, alcoholism, drug abuse, or physical abuse.

Ministering to couples with great needs requires a lot of teamwork between you and your spouse. Listen to your partner. Together God will give you more wisdom and skill in ministering than you can imagine.

What if someone doesn't want to be in the group?

Expect some people, especially husbands, to arrive at the first session wishing they were someplace else. Some will be there just because their spouse or another couple nagged them to come. Some may be suspicious of a Bible study. Others may be fearful of revealing any weaknesses in their marriage. And some may feel either that their marriage is beyond help or that they don't need any help.

You can eliminate a great deal of anxiety and resistance at the first session. Simply begin by mentioning that you know there are probably some who came reluctantly. Share a few reasons people may feel that way, and affirm that regardless of why anyone has come, you are pleased each person is there.

Briefly comment on how the concepts in this study have helped you and your marriage, and express your confidence that each person will enjoy the study and benefit from it. Also assure the group that at no time will anyone be forced to share publicly. What each person shares is his or her choice; no one will be embarrassed.

Privately thank God for bringing a reluctant person into your group and seek to get to know the person during the early weeks of the study. God may use you to change his or her life forever.

How can I get everyone to participate in the group discussion?

Ask God to give you sensitivity in dealing with this issue. First, remember you shouldn't force anyone to respond to a question; you promised in the first session that you wouldn't do that.

Second, remember that many people who hardly open their mouths in early sessions will become more comfortable the longer you meet. If you sense someone is not participating primarily because of insecurity over answering questions about Bible verses, you may find a natural way in later sessions to ask him or her to answer questions calling for an opinion or a personal experience.

One of the best ways to generate greater participation is to utilize subgroups. Particularly if your group is large, we encourage you to divide into subgroups of about three couples for the Blueprints questions.

When someone who doesn't usually share says something, you may want to give encouragement by expressing what a good point that was. Remember the point and refer back to it, saying, "Like Jim said..." That type of comment usually encourages a person to participate more regularly.

Another problem related to participation is that some people direct their answers to the leader rather than to the group as a whole. We've found that one remedy for this problem is to avoid maintaining eye contact with that person as he or she talks. Look at that person for a few moments, and then look away if you have to. This simple action often leads the person to look around at others in the group.

How do I handle the overly talkative person?

Here are two ideas:

1. Sit next to that person. That may help him or her be a bit more quiet.

2. Let this person lead a session or part of one sometime. If you try this, make sure you emphasize the necessity to guide the discussion rather than teach the material. Explain to the talkative person beforehand how important it is to get others participating. He or she will get the idea and may start being a big help to you.

How can I make sure all the material gets covered?

Once the people in your group get to know one another and interaction gets under way, you may find it difficult to complete a session in the time allotted. That's why it's important to decide beforehand which questions you definitely want to cover.

If you are pressed for time, be careful to avoid making comments about time pressure that will make the group feel rushed. Here are some suggestions:

- When you need to move the discussion to the next item, say something like, "We could probably talk about that question the rest of the evening, but we need to consider several other important questions on this issue."

- If you see that you won't cover all the questions, when you're out of time simply say, "You can see that there are several more questions we could have moved on to discuss, but I felt we were making real progress, so I chose to spend extra time on the earlier points."

- When the group is unable to come to a conclusion, remind them that one goal is to begin meaningful conversations among couples that will continue throughout the week, not necessarily to answer every question that session.

What if someone has strongly different views from those in Scripture?

Keep the focus on what Scripture says, not on you, your ideas, or those of the group members. When someone disagrees with Scripture, affirm him or her for wrestling with the issue and point out that some biblical statements are hard to understand or to accept. Encourage the person to keep an open mind on the issue at least through the remainder of the study. Don't bring in other Scriptures to refute the person in front of the group. If necessary, make an appointment to share additional Scriptures with this person privately.

Avoid labeling an answer as wrong. Doing so can kill the atmosphere for discussion. Encourage a person who gives an unbiblical or incomplete answer to look again at the question or the Scripture being explored. Encourage others to look for further insights by making comments such as, "What else do you see here?" or "Any additional ideas?"

How do you handle someone who keeps bringing up certain topics that don't apply to the session?

Some Christians have a particular interest in biblical prophecy, in certain theological issues, or in controversial cultural issues. After several sessions you may notice that someone tends to steer the group discussion to such a topic. The first step is to put the discussion back on track—perhaps by repeating the question or by moving to the next one. If this doesn't work, talk to the person outside the group meeting and ask him or her to avoid talking about that particular subject.

How can I establish an environment of accountability?

From the outset, emphasize the importance of completing the HomeBuilders Project after each session. These projects give couples the opportunity to discuss what they've learned and apply it to their lives. The couples who complete these projects will get much more out of the study than those who do not.

One of the most important things you can do is state at the end of the first session that at your next meeting you will ask each couple to share something they learned from the HomeBuilders Project. Then at the next session follow through on your promise. If they know you're going to hold them accountable, they'll be more motivated to complete the projects. And they'll be very glad they did! Remember, though, to make this an environment of *friendly* accountability. Emphasize how beneficial the projects are and how much couples will grow in their marriages if they faithfully complete them. But be careful not to make those who don't complete the projects feel less a part of the group. Often the projects are too stressful for couples experiencing marriage problems. Just remaining part of the group may be all a couple can handle.

Also, keep in mind that an important part of leading is setting an example. Be sure that you and your spouse faithfully complete the projects as well.

During Sunday school a young couple shared that their five-year-old marriage had been going through hard times. I appreciated their honesty and vulnerability to share their hearts and struggles with their peers.

Having just completed the HomeBuilders study Building Your Marriage, *they said, "This study saved our marriage and gave us new hope, as well as a blueprint to live by." They concluded by saying, "Now we have hope."*

Barry and Jeannie Steger

Chapter Six

Using HomeBuilders for Outreach

Nothing is more important in life than establishing a relationship with Jesus Christ and responding by faith to his gift of forgiveness for our sins. In fact, trying to build a good marriage without a vital, intimate relationship with Jesus Christ is like trying to build a house on shifting sand. Men and women must have the solid foundation of faith in God to realize all that he can do for their marriages.

After we spoke at a marriage seminar in Lexington, Kentucky, a man wrote on a comment card, "You make it sound like you can't have the best marriage unless you are a Christian." I guess we made that clear!

In our culture, the issue of family is one of the best platforms for reaching people with the gospel of Christ. Many others, who may already know Christ, can have their spiritual lives refreshed as you reach out to them with a HomeBuilders Bible study. Bill Bright, founder and president of Campus Crusade for Christ, has said, "If you reach the family, you will reach the world."

Principles taught in HomeBuilders materials lay out God's blueprints for marriage and family in a way that addresses the critical needs in families. Men and women are interested because they're looking for answers. When we "scratch where it itches," people respond. And HomeBuilders is an excellent way to do this.

Tips for leading an outreach group

1. *Create a nonthreatening environment.* This type of group is best done in a home setting rather than at church.

Your openness in telling about your own experiences and mistakes in marriage is another key ingredient to creating a nonthreatening environment. This will help couples feel more comfortable and less defensive.

2. *Have fun!* HomeBuilders is strong medicine for many couples. Make friends and encourage laughter to break the tension. Couples having fun are more likely to put the lessons into practice and to continue coming. In fact, having fun together is often more important than finishing all the questions.

3. *Be patient.* Some couples may state some very nonbiblical ideas. Don't correct them. For example, if someone says something like, "God led me to get divorced," don't stop and say, "Well, the Bible says that God hates divorce, so how could he possibly lead you to get one?" Instead, continue on with the HomeBuilders study. Let God's Spirit use your example and the Scriptures in HomeBuilders to touch the hearts of others. (For example, if someone says, "Do you think God leads people to get divorced?" this is an indication that he or she may have an open heart, and you can take the opportunity to lead them to appropriate Scriptures at a later time.)

4. *Be flexible.* These couples are precious to God. If necessary, sacrifice your own convenience to arrange meeting times, child care, and so on, for them.

5. *Don't let Christians who may join your group "witness" to your couples in a confrontational or condescending manner.* Avoid at all costs a "them-and-us" division between Christians and non-Christians in the group.

6. *Respect privacy.* Nothing will anger some couples more than hearing that people ouside the group are praying for them. If this happens, they will know you've been talking about them outside the group. Keep what is shared in your group private. In an outreach group, you may even want to keep the names of the people private.

7. *Start and end on time.* Many people feel uncomfortable with too much small talk at the beginning of the session if they don't know the others well. Also, the topics studied will be painful for some. Don't extend the sessions or they may not return.

8. *Work together as a team.* Realize your spouse may be more in tune to a need in the group than you are. Discuss who needs encouragement, for example, regularly with your spouse.

9. *Avoid embarrassing anyone.* Many people have little Bible knowledge. For example, don't call on someone to read unless you're certain they've found the verse.

10. *Don't force people to talk.* This point is even more important in an outreach group than in a group consisting of Christians.

Presenting the gospel

As non-Christians begin to see how the Bible applies to their marriage, many will begin developing an interest in spiritual things. It's critical that they clearly understand their need for a personal relationship with Christ.

There are several ways to present the gospel. Ask God for discernment on how to approach the person.

1. *Share what God has done in your life.* Since HomeBuilders is designed to be a group discussion, telling what God has done in your life is a very natural and easy way to share the gospel during a session. Your story of faith is one of the best gifts you can give your group. Your story will personalize the gospel by showing its reality in a person's life in a manner that cannot be refuted or argued. You are an authority on what God has done for you. Also, if you have never done this, preparing to share will help you develop a clearer understanding of how God brought you to himself.

Remember that your main objective is to communicate in such a way that others will know how to trust Christ. Do not be concerned that your story is exciting or dramatic, just that it's real. If possible, try to build it around the single theme of how Christ has changed your life. For example, tell how your personal goals or relationships with others have changed.

The Scripture gives an example of an effective faith story by Paul in Acts 26:1-23. Your testimony probably won't be as dramatic as Paul's, but it can contain the same three elements:

• *Your life before you met Christ.* Begin with an attention-grabbing statement, question, or story. Then tell what attitudes characterized your life before you became a Christian.

• *Your faith commitment experience.* Relate what happened in your life that changed your thoughts, attitudes, or misconceptions about Christianity. Be specific about what you did to receive Christ. What you did is more important than when or where you did it.

• *Your life after making a commitment to Christ.* Explain the changes that God began making in your life. Be sure that the changes you communicate relate to attitudes and actions mentioned earlier when describing your life before

Christ. Briefly explain what your relationship with Christ means to you now. You may also want to share a Scripture verse that is meaningful to you.

Sample Faith Story

Everyone said I was a good kid. I made good grades, went to Sunday school, and said "Yes, sir" and "No, ma'am" to my elders. I went away to college and things were about the same. I was on the dean's list, had a car, a job, and a girlfriend. Everyone said I had it made.

But inside I knew otherwise. For one thing, I lay awake at night wondering what would happen to me when I died. I had a terrible temper and would throw and break things when I didn't get my way. Worst of all, I used people to get what I wanted. As a result, I didn't have any real friends, only acquaintances.

A guy I had gone to high school with invited me to attend a Bible study. The topic was how to know you are a Christian. One part I remember was, "And this is the testimony: God has given us eternal life, and this life is in his Son. He who has the Son has life; he who does not have the Son of God does not have life (1 John 5:11-12)." I knew that I didn't have either Jesus Christ or eternal life.

Previously, I had a vague idea that God had a balance scale in heaven. He would put the good things on one side and the bad things on the other. Whichever way it went would determine where I would spend eternity. But I couldn't know which way until I got there.

I started to ask a lot of questions. I asked, "Where did Cain get his wife?" and "How did Noah get all the animals on the ark?" I never got all the answers, but I became convinced by the character of the Bible study leaders that Jesus Christ is real and that he could change my life.

One night in the privacy of my dorm room I prayed a prayer something like this, "Jesus, I know I have sinned against you. Thank you for dying on the cross for my sins. Please come into my life to be my Lord and Savior. Make me the kind of person you want me to be." And immediately I felt...nothing. I didn't feel any different. But I knew that Jesus would keep his promise and had come into my life.

Very soon my life started to change. First, I didn't have to worry about what would happen to me when I died. Then I learned to trust God in many situations, and my temper improved. Then God taught me how to really care for other people, and soon I had the kind of friends I'd always wanted.

I'm still a long way from being Mr. Perfect. And I never will be. But I know that everything I have, everything I am, and everything I will ever be, I owe to what my Lord Jesus Christ has done for me.

2. *Invite them to church.* You will develop close relationships with the couples in your HomeBuilders group. As your friends, they are much more likely to attend your church or an event where the gospel is clearly presented. If possible, attend together. Their knowledge of what God has done in your life beforehand will help prepare their hearts.

3. *Set a private appointment.* In many cases it works best to schedule a private meeting to present the message of Christ. We suggest setting these meetings individually—

husband to husband and wife to wife; this is one of the advantages of developing a ministry as a husband and wife team. Many men are reluctant to expose their lack of spiritual understanding in front of their wives.

Sometime during the course of the study, schedule a time to meet with this person or couple. Pray before meeting them, confessing any known sin in your own life, and asking God to prepare their hearts. If only one member of the leadership couple goes to the appointment, the other can pray during that time. If both of you attend, the one who is not sharing should continue in silent prayer.

At your meeting, begin in a friendly manner, but quickly move to the reason you wanted to meet. Otherwise you may use all of your time visiting. You can say something like, "An important part of HomeBuilders is each person's relationship with God. Would you allow me to take a few minutes to cover the way HomeBuilders uses the Bible to direct both husbands and wives to God?" If the answer is yes, explain the gospel and offer an opportunity to make a commitment of faith in Christ. We recommend using the article, "Our Problems, God's Answers" that is in every HomeBuilders study.

If a couple isn't ready to make a faith commitment, assure them that you want them to continue with the group, and continue to pray for them.

Following up with those who make a faith commitment

One great thing about using HomeBuilders as a platform to present the gospel is that those who make a faith commitment to Christ are already in a Bible study. If a new Christian is interested, begin meeting to study some of the basics of the Christian life. One good exercise to recommend to a new Christian is to read through the Gospel of John.

Some other resources we recommend include *Five Steps of Christian Growth* by Bill Bright, the *"JESUS"* film video (available from Campus Crusade for Christ), and the *Growing Together in Christ* HomeBuilders study by David Sunde.

Don't give new Christians a list of things to change in their lives. Trust the Holy Spirit to convict them through his Word. Encourage them to continue in HomeBuilders and, if they don't already have a church, suggest several they might try.

●

After doing two different HomeBuilders Couples Series Bible studies with our neighbors, I finally realized that I had been doing battle with Christ and I was losing. I gave up the fight and asked for God's grace and forgiveness. I recommitted my life to Christ. God truly is forgiving, for Kathy and I do not deserve the grace God has shown our family. We have since led several HomeBuilders studies in our neighborhood. Our goal is to strengthen marriages by sharing our life experiences and our faith in Christ with others. The HomeBuilders Bible study has been a wonderful tool we've used to achieve that goal.

Terry and Kathy Shoemaker

Chapter Seven

Expanding Your HomeBuilders Ministry

There is nothing more exciting than seeing God work in and through you to have an impact on your neighborhood, your church, your community, and even on the world. Over the years we've seen thousands of couples experience this excitement through their involvement with HomeBuilders. And an increasing number have caught a vision that is even more intoxicating—how they can be involved in the Great Commission by expanding their HomeBuilders ministry.

Making disciples

Do you feel God wants you to reach out to families? One of the most effective ways to have a tremendous impact on your world is to multiply your ministry by training disciples—couples who will start HomeBuilders groups of their own.

In Matthew 28:19-20, Jesus told his disciples, "Therefore go and make disciples of all nations, baptizing them in the name of the Father and of the Son and of the Holy Spirit, and teaching them to obey everything I have commanded you. And surely I am with you always, to the very end of the age."

Jesus spent most of his time with a small group of men—his disciples—during his ministry on earth. He taught them, encouraged them, and sent them out on outreach assignments. And after his resurrection and ascension, this group of men went out and changed the world.

This is called multiplication—training disciples who will go out and train others. It's the same principle Paul teaches in 2 Timothy 2:2: "And the things you have heard me say in the presence of many witnesses entrust to reliable men who will also be qualified to teach others."

We conduct leadership training for couples who want to begin a HomeBuilders movement in their community. One couple came to a conference and expressed their disappointment with the group they had led. "Nobody wanted to do another one," the wife said. "We don't belong at your leadership conference."

They were surprised to learn that a couple from their defunct HomeBuilders group was there also. This couple turned out to be one of the most active HomeBuilders coordinators in their state. And this couple had brought another couple that had already led several groups.

The original couple—that was so disappointed in the response of their group—had actually spawned at least three generations of multiplication and never knew it! They left the conference pretty excited about how God had used them.

As a movement grows, no person really runs or directs it, or even knows all that is going on. The movement belongs to God. Once we spoke to a group of couples about attending the FamilyLife Marriage Conference. Their response was, "That sounds pretty good. But have you guys heard about HomeBuilders studies? They're really terrific." We assured them that we knew that HomeBuilders was great and politely left. In the car, we burst out laughing. We realized they were our fifth generation disciples in HomeBuilders, and they didn't even know us. That is our greatest joy in ministry—meeting couples God has touched through our ministry who don't even know who we are.

Training new HomeBuilders leaders

As you form and lead your group, ask God to raise up a couple who shares your vision for reaching out to families. Look for people who demonstrate faithfulness, teachability, and availability. When you become aware of such a couple, ask them to help you with the group.

Start by challenging them beforehand to read a few of the questions during a session. Ask them to guide that portion of the discussion. Next, have them facilitate half of a group session. Afterward, privately discuss with them how they did, and be as encouraging as possible.

If you have to be absent, have them lead an entire session instead of postponing the session. Again, discuss the results with them later.

As you near the end of your current study, invite them to lead an entire session. And after it's over, challenge them to start their own group. If they agree, work with them to evaluate how and where to form their group. However, don't be disappointed if they don't start a group right away. Frequently, there is a delay of several years between training and putting it into practice. Young couples with growing families in particular may need to delay their service. If you are patient, loving, and don't pressure your disciples, they will help reach other families when they are able. One couple we encouraged waited eight years before starting a very dynamic HomeBuilders ministry to young couples.

Additional expansion strategies

1. Meet with pastors at other churches to encourage them to start HomeBuilders groups. You can tell them about the benefits of HomeBuilders in a church. Perhaps most important, offer to train and coach couples in their churches to lead HomeBuilders groups. We tell pastors, "We are your free consultant to families."

2. Meet with other couples who desire to start HomeBuilders groups to provide training and encouragement. If the FamilyLife Marriage Conference is held in your area, contact the city ministry director to find out if any couples need help to get their groups going.

3. Offer "group start" assistance: Often couples want to start a HomeBuilders group in their church or among their friends and neighbors, but they aren't certain how a group should be conducted. You can go and lead the first session, then turn it over to the leader couple.

4. Organize HomeBuilders orientations and training. We have developed material for anything from a one-hour to a one-day training seminar that you can hold in your community. For help in organizing this type of training, call FamilyLife at 1-800-FL-TODAY and ask for the HomeBuilders office.

We joined a HomeBuilders group a few months after we became
Christians. We were probably every leader's nightmare.
We kept firing off questions left and right. But the group helped us
grow in our new faith.

During one group meeting, the leader told us that the ultimate goal
of the study was to divide and multiply. He challenged us to
lead groups of our own. We thought, "We are in the wrong place if we
need to lead one of these groups."

But two years later, we were challenged again, and this time we
decided to lead a group. We did this for three years.

At our church we saw a glaring need for ministry to couples as a unit.
There were programs for women, men, youth, the needy, international
students, and singles, but nothing for married couples. We went to the
leadership and told them that we strongly felt that the Lord had
brought us here to establish HomeBuilders groups in this church.

We made an announcement to the church right after a
FamilyLife Marriage Conference in our area. Seven couples signed up
to be leaders. Then we ended up with forty-five couples who were ready
and willing to be placed in HomeBuilders groups.

Bob and Kerri Cole

Exciting Resources for Your Adult Ministry!

The Dirt on Learning
Thom & Joani Schultz

This thought-provoking book explores what Jesus' Parable of the Sower says about effective teaching *and* learning. Readers will rethink the Christian education methods used in their churches and consider what really works. Use the video training kit to challenge and inspire your entire ministry team and set a practical course of action for Christian education methods that really *work!*

ISBN 0-7644-2088-7   Book Only
ISBN 0-7644-2152-2   Video Training Kit

The Family-Friendly Church
Ben Freudenburg with Rick Lawrence

Discover how certain programming can often short-circuit your church's ability to truly strengthen families—and what you can do about it! You'll get practical ideas and suggestions featuring profiles of real churches. It also includes thought-provoking application worksheets that will help you apply the principles and insights to your own church.

ISBN 0-7644-2048-8

Disciple-Making Teachers
Josh Hunt with Dr. Larry Mays

This clear, practical guide equips teachers of adult classes to have impact—and produce disciples eager for spiritual growth and ministry. You get a Bible-based, proven process that's achieved results in churches like yours—and comes highly recommended by Christian leaders like Dr. Bruce Wilkinson, Findley Edge, and Robert Coleman. Discover what needs to happen before class through preparation, in class during teaching, and after class in service to turn your adult classes into disciple groups.

ISBN 0-7644-2031-3

Extraordinary Results From Ordinary Teachers
Michael D. Warden

Now both professional *and* volunteer Christian educators can teach as Jesus taught! You'll explore the teaching style and methods of Jesus and get clear and informed ways to deepen your teaching and increase your impact! This is an essential resource for every teacher, youth worker, or pastor.

ISBN 0-7644-2013-5

Discover our full line of children's, youth, and adult ministry resources at your local Christian bookstore, or write: Group Publishing, P.O. Box 485, Loveland, CO 80539. www.grouppublishing.com

*S*ince attending a FamilyLife Marriage Conference, the Martins' love really shows...

But who's keeping score?

FAMILYLIFE MARRIAGE CONFERENCE
Get away for a "Weekend to Remember"!

Chalk one up for your marriage! Get away to a FamilyLife Marriage Conference for a fun, meaningful weekend together. Learn how to understand your mate, build your marriage, and much more.

To register or receive more information,
visit www.familylife.com or call 1-800-FL-TODAY.

FAMILYLIFE™
Bringing Timeless Principles Home

Make Your Marriage the Best It Can Be!

Great marriages don't just happen—husbands and wives need to nurture them. They need to make their marriage relationship a priority.

That's where the newly revised HomeBuilders Couples Series® can help! The series consists of interactive 6- to 7-week small group studies that make it *easy* for couples to really open up with each other. The result is fun, non-threatening interactions that build stronger Christ-centered relationships between spouses—*and* with other couples!

Whether you've been married for years, or are newly married, this series will help you and your spouse discover timeless principles from God's Word that you can apply to your marriage and make it the best it can be!

The HomeBuilders Couples Series includes these life-changing studies:
HomeBuilders Leader Guide
Building Teamwork in Your Marriage
Building Your Marriage
Building Your Mate's Self-Esteem
Growing Together in Christ
Improving Communication in Your Marriage
Making Your Remarriage Last
Mastering Money in Your Marriage
Overcoming Stress in Your Marriage
Raising Children of Faith
Resolving Conflict in Your Marriage

Look for the **HomeBuilders Couples Series** at your local Christian bookstore or write:

P.O. Box 485, Loveland, CO 80539.
www.grouppublishing.com

Bringing Timeless Principles Home

www.familylife.com